AmeriModern

POEMS

First printing July 1982
Library of Congress number 81-75785
ISBNs 0-943096-02-2 and 0-943096-03-0

To reproduce parts of this book, write to:

HART'S SPRING WORKS P.O. Box 1609, Suite 200
533 Sutter Street
San Francisco, California 94102

**Distributed by L-S Distributors in San Francisco,
Book Dynamics in New York City, and
Baker & Taylor of Somerville, New Jersey.**

CONTENTS

AmeriModern

Our—

Bodies undergoing
Fast mutation,
Spread in lines, com-
Pact with dispossessions
From the U.S.
Casting into every
Heart, every brain and
"Ev'ry eye-eye-I . . ."

(With
the spurious
perk of a
Pop jingle:
"A-mer-i-modern
It
Does Things
For You!")

—America! Oh, how,
In years of finned plenty,
Child chests swelled with singing you!
Now—

Oh, poor, brute, stripped
Superreaper, once past measuring—
What's happened? "What's happening?"
We here fear to tell
Our souls' knowing.

To whom, to what
Does our vast home lost belong?
Unbounded business!
Beyond nationality, loyal to profit only,
Economies turn 'Nature' under stamps;
As Ages ago, they for *usura* order.
Polyfabs. suiting 'Progress',
Surfacing comforts, feeding well-fleshed and
(As needs must) lean,
Uproot, sell out, senses of our selves,
Claims and territories once open taken,

In a long-going, one-upon-another scheme.

Is this
One's prophecy of the Eagle from iron Angels
          rending free?
Or is it the all for each in the States declared,
Carried by patriots' and immigrants' hungers
Through Wars and frontiers as keying their destiny,
Sustained by poets' celebrations too?
          No! Nay— "No!" now.
          Look at how
          We like cattle serve, stalled,
          Within some borderless, runaway, greedily
                    devouring Thing.

          Shaped bodies! Used buyers!
          Split as schedules rife,
          Consuming and of course consumed,
          Bent to disillusion
          Yet bound to loving home,
          What have *we*?

A Tour

LOOK!
Look at spectacles of these States, corrupted alike,
          At things indivisible with our selves.

   You might begin with travelers' sightseeing.
   Railroads, old lines, bedded upon the public
Trust by lordly thieves of their Age, crisscross
The nation still, rapes become romantic rusting.
   Go, swaying car drawn faster behind diesel bulls,
By bridges black'ned in Harlem, Buffalo, Cleveland,

Detroit, Chicago, Bessemer, El Paso, Tacoma, . . . ,
By mills like gated cities for giant alchemy.
   Or on concrete of the System you can roll
By cool, secluded quarries of northern Colonies—
Hear the "bah" where "a's" are given "r's"—
By the combustible Cuyahoga and waste-steeped Lakes,
Through Hills and Cuts and Gaps ('See Ruby Falls!')
Of green for marveling.
   Either way west soon reaches fields—oh, *days* of
Fields, undulant, colors-checked and outstretched,
Flattening horizons but under sunlight vibrant,
Breathing of fertility between Winter's freeze,
Across the Middle West and Prairie, where AM
Stations congratulate the newly married.
   Here you may see hands on combines mowing swaths,
Harvesting corporations' crops nitrates-nutrified.
They can tell you what happened to the family's farm,
The same as pieceworkers back East will about shops.
   Farther, beyond yards and stock ranging wide—
Oh, hard lines binding cowboys' ride—round
Mountains bristling with forests and more mysterious
In clouds, behind the sunset noctilucence of
Deserts and of buttes, under theater of the Big Sky
That may hours hang your jaw, to fog-limbed bluffs and
Bays of coasts, where there's nowhere else to go,
You'll have company known since the start.
Smoke
Hazes cinerally,
Inseparable with mill, mine, factory, refinery, . . . ,
Like a smear of feces
Round city and town,
Its seeping soiling scarred into every eye.

   You might go CLOSER—into how we're housed.
   Old rows of stone and brick and wood, stooped

Tenements and flat frames, in and outlying city
Grids, ingrain the grime of factories.
    Blunter yet, between "the train" and cracked
Freeways, Projects isolate blocks in the forsaken
Bronx, Chicago, New Orleans, ..., their
Prison-dismal shades slashed by scrawls, ("It
Junk shot to be high, free of nodding   does things
Courts, where kids whirl with basketballs.   to you.")
    Toward sun-baked spaces trailer camps, more
Modern ranks, sprung round booming, fuming Evanston,
Odessa, Lafayette, ..., extend the lines,
Aerials accessory to new migrants brought by
"Money" to meet the nation's 'Needs' for power.
    And flying into Los Angeles or ..., you may see
That suburbs of shells-with-lawns spread below
Resemble the cartons of aluminum ranked above—
Or that these communities are like compacted gravel—
Or like chips of microcompressing silicon flung, and
That commuters' cars, grayed beads shuttling through
The network strung, may not be distinguished
From all the Homes and Plants, Malls and ...
            "And we gaze out on,
            And we gaze out on, ... "
            A-mer-i-Modern!

Such lines—rails and mills,
Fields and Shores, tenements, Projects,
Camps and " 'burbs", these Walks of
Marts and Drives of Heights (Shop by Phone)—
'R they *ours*?
No! "This is not a real home."
        Don't you want to cry,
        Cry at how we're kept, then fight,
        Fight against such death-in-life?

Seers earlier,
One imagining that Revolution's Demon might leave
        the Guardian overthrown,
A later—broad—holding to the States beside
        death's endless envelopment,
Would surely cry at this rape as we sleep.
And compatriots racked against our century,
Suffering too much to sing from the founding dream
Save in keenly wrought lament,
Would jump again at visions more set.
                New latitudes, defined, have given place,
                Deranging private space!
                Mated with mediocrity, servilely we
                Slide, stuck in a desolating peace,
                Our dreams stopped and split
                By heads' still rough-and-ready talk
                Of winning holocausts!

    Five years ago I was riding the Sunset Limited
and a woman from Indiana, traveling the country
with her daughter, looked across tracks to the
border as the train rocked into El Paso. She said,
    "Beautiful buildings and poor, poor people."

We, become more of a "poor, poor people"
Too—
                Hurt most by what
                We fear to tell
                But can't help taking in—
Know we're being raped,
Raped in our sleep.
                And isn't it time to WAKE UP,
                Wake up to our life,
                Stand up for a fight?

7

March 3, 1982
First version 3/'77

Rubber Soul

Oh, innocence!
How little I knew
About the world outside high school;
Too little about 'Vietnam' etc.
For suspicions to be proved.
The Beatles were singing—
" ...told that girl that my prospects were good":
"I once met a girl, or should I say ... "—
And nearly everybody who heard
Could really dance.

Such a rush from that past
Throws me back,
As I happen on this album
Already nine years old
In the stack of a woman my age, upstate
New York, cross-country from where I was raised,
Those four in black focused as round a stamen,
Faces still fresh and hair not yet "hippie" long.
And, oh, with the songs
What wondering, plangent nostalgia
For our forgotten, ignorant innocence.

March 4, 1982
First version 11/'75

Rocked in a Current

Dreaming through Sunday after a night up and
Still pulled into dreams the next day—
I met again at friends' crowded party,
Dancing past midnight,
The "girlfriend" of a professor I like though
    hardly know—
I want but doubt. Pleasurably
Musing steals and wraps around me, swaying,
Infusing headily, like a chemical.

"It would be a disaster," I think aloud.
Dawn noticed all at once, we three and a few
More "hard core" sat around the kitchen table.
Laughing, she said, "You're so romantic."
Everybody except us, even Henry the stolidly
    providing black-belt,
Took to rest. We cleaned up. Then I caught
Her on a walk. Our talk was to be revealing.
And how we started, eyes surprised, happening to
Meet as she and he left!
But I think, "The trouble, the trouble."

Then—why should that matter? The unreasoning
Current—of incalculable aspects: faces, figures,
Glances of alike mirrors attracting, as deeper parts
(Character, say) intimate what might be—
Grabs and dizzies me, fog of hangover past for cause,
Like a swell to the blood that's
Then—alas!—kept in the head.

March 4, 1982
First version 4/'76

The Ducking

Carrying lunches and rain gear, Norvel, Jerry and I walked with sluggish, jolting steps far down the hill to start the morning. Stiff but warming and limbering up, we set chokers around logs the first few turns. The clear, ideal air was about freezing. The ground was frozen. Shaded patches of frosted snow left after hard raining Monday and Tuesday spotted the variegated green brush. We were deep in the canyon toward the creek after logging almost all January. Clouds vaulted over the sky between spaces of blue. We were isolated. The scene was grand. The four logs that we choked last rose uphill under the high, tightened, spooling main-line of the Skagit yarder about two thousand feet away, its one-hundred-foot round white tower hidden though no clinging fog rolled between us and the landing. Ends of the logs nosed and kicked the brown earth "road" made in places that yarded logs scraped regularly.

A whizzing like a tremendous blade cutting down startled us from dullness. We crouched and ducked behind cover. The main-line—one-and-a-half inches of stranded steel thick—of this slack-line show fell. Whizz-*ooosh*—Crack! It slapped along the ground off beside us. We erected. "Fuck!" Norvel Rogers, the small, sturdy, longhaired blond rigging slinger a year younger than me, said. "She's gone again, boys." "Did it break again?" "Did you hear that motherfucker *falling*? It sounded like *death*," exclaimed Jerry Umdall, the other choker setter, taller than us, ragged holes in his leather cork boots and faded but blackened Boss of the Road rigging pants. We took our time in climbing out.

On the landing Jack Presley, the hook tender, said, "Nah, I think the tail-hold pulled." He smiled after speaking with knowing what he told. He bossed the Van de Grift gypo crew in the woods. Strong at about 5'10", features big on his hard and prominent face, teeth especially big, his blue eyes deep in their sockets, commanding when they lighted, hard as a rule but softly boylike when he was uncertain, his face toughened but blanching, whiskers thinning on his cheeks and chin at age forty-seven, a logger since 1955, one of families of Tarheels around Sedro Wooley and eastward towns neighboring the Cascade Mountains, Jack was said to be one of the few good slack-line hook tenders around, said by Norvel and Jerry to win $500 some Saturday nights playing 4-5-6 in the tavern in Lyman that he used to own. Norvel, Jerry, Irv and I cussed at what Jack said, I cussing softly.

A lot of work was ahead. Except Wayne running the yarder for us, Archie the loader for trucks on the landing, and Jack carrying tools, we all had to pack ninety-pound coils down to the creek and then a thousand feet uphill on the other side to lay out whatever new tail-hold Jack found. "I just *knew* this was going to be a shitty day," Irv, the chaser, said in his quite high voice. Short, burly, shaved black beard clear on his face, his eyes small, he unsnapped the iron bells and knobs of chokers around logs on the landing with one hand. "At least it'll get you off your dead ass up here," Norvel said. "What d'you mean, *my dead ass*, you little shit," Irv began.

At first we rested together. Frosted mud in the road slipped out under our cork boots and stuck to them. We crossed back and forth along the draw of a rivulet, icicles dripping to it, and climbed around rock bluffs. The coil of quarter-inch "haywire" dug into my shoulder and grazed my neck as I tilted away from its weight. Jack and Norvel drew farther ahead between stops. After the second-to-last bluff we walked with relief over a plateau. We hit the part that we hadn't logged yet and fought brush around logs.

Trudging along them, wobbling, bending tough and swatting fir and hemlock branches, twisting around knotted stubs, aiming after Jack's and Norvel's course, I grew violently irritated. My lunch bucket in one hand with its one broken snap kept opening. I cussed it. I felt like crying, weeping at the stupid, demeaning labor and my frustration. The work and day no longer pleased me. As I bent to get around a fir branch to the bucked end of another log, the coil slipped off my shoulder down into the brush.

"Goddamn it! Fuck! Son of a bitch! Son of a bitch!" "What happened?" Jerry called. "Aw, he's just throwin' one of his tantrums again," Irv said. I hated him. I felt persecuted because we hadn't left our lunches or "nosebags" before starting into the unlogged brush. Irv packed a small 10" block with his coil. I said I could take the block for a while. "No, I can get it," he said.

He passed me after I lost the coil again below the last bluff. Sighing, whimpering, infuriated and stumbling, I wound between pools on marshy ground in nearing the creek. I wanted to impress the crew.

It was to be my fourth-to-last day with them. Christmas day when Jack called me to go back to work, I said I had to leave at the end of January. I told him again Monday morning. We were paid for 9 hours a day Monday through Saturday. Driving from Bellingham, I picked up Jerry outside his parents' trailer-house in Alger. Jerry's second wife left him just before Christmas. He was twenty-six. He spent a year in Vietnam as a helicopter mechanic. He wanted to get a hot car before buying new cork boots. At 6:00 Jack with Norvel in one Van de Grift crummie picked us up. We rode an hour and a half each way to the show up a Forest Service spur-road into Canyon Creek above Granite Falls. Spattering rain usually swished across the windshield as we rode on the freeway and roads. At about 7:30 Jack let us off in darkness again.

Norvel said, "I go home and don't know if I'm looking at the wall or the TV. My wife starts jerking on my arm, all excited about something, and I nod, 'Uh-huh.' " Norvel got married the past October. His nineteen-year-old wife was due to make him a papa in June. He went into the woods at seventeen after quitting high school. All but a few times he was fastest in climbing out when Wayne blew us off at 5:30. Norvel repeated, sang and came up with lines and limericks that I thought were clever. What most oppressed me with him as with all of them at work was having nothing to say.

By the rushing creek Norvel smoked another cigarette that he rolled with Bugler tobacco to save money, Jack another Winston, Irv sitting next to them on rocks. Jerry came after me. It was past 11:00. Getting down about 3,000 feet with the coils took us over two hours. Sipping icy water from my tin hat, sweat drying in the cool air, I felt alive and re-strengthened. The creek was a lot higher and wider with rains and snow than when we last saw it in early January. "It was hardly more than a trickle. Now it's something like a river," Irv said. The current flowing in its middle a transparent green color, it ran into shallow rapids down from us. Sharp blue showed in larger spaces between cumulous clouds. We rested over fifteen minutes.

Someone had to climb across on the haywire strung over the creek between tree trunks, then "yard" across the first of the others, who would ride on a branch under a pulley. The rope to yard on angled from the haywire to the other bank. Norvel, Irv and Jerry had climbed across weeks ago, but not after packing a coil. If they could do it, I could, I thought.

We four agreed that it was my turn, happy and relieved to have got the coils this far, but waited for Jack to say definitely. He stared ahead with his eyes and mouth set thoughtfully. He and I affected each other. We were alike but far apart. We were like a distantly different father and son who nevertheless affected each other to the quick at moments. I sometimes felt to him as toward a father. I believe he called me "son" as more than as a logger's familiar pejorative. We got on each other's nerves sharply. We disappointed each other easily. We looked something alike. We were self-willed. We worried about each

other. We talked to each other only with strain. Our intimate
connection came out only in flashes. He was a tough, long-
time hook tender, a Tarheel not very educated, proud, sensi-
tive, living near Sedro Wooley. I was a green choker-setter
from a town twenty miles north that had the airs of a city to
him. Guys from there had not talked to him when he worked
for Washington Loggers. I most wanted to impress Jack, he
the focus for me among them. "You better be sure you make
it," Jack said. "I have to make it," I said with a somewhat forced
laugh.

Feet first,
Rain coat, mackinaw, rubber gloves off,
I scooted. Then the pushing got harder.
The haywire curved up. I stopped, oversized
Rubber cork boots to the angling rope
Unforeseen, the creek rushing below
My marsupial hanging. "Get on top of it!"
Irv shouted. No. I would drop my legs and
Get around. Pulling with my hands might be
Easier, too. But with legs dropped I could
Not pull my weight. So I dangled, stopped
At the rope, only fifteen feet or so to go.
"Get on top of it! Get on top of it!" they
Advised more urgently behind me. Raise
Your legs and go like before, I thought,
Still sure of making it. I raised them
Halfway—no more. With muscles quivering,
Grip to the haywire hurting, I realized
Timelessly that I had nowhere to go.
Will wouldn't work. Despite danger and shame,
I could only let go.
No! Yep.
Falling the over ten feet to the creek fast,
The blur of a bomb but with arms and legs
Spread-eagled—red, blue and yellow patches

on my cork's like a clown's—I plunged under
The snow-fed water, popped up in a semi-eddy,
And, driving, stroking, flailing, scrambled
To the bank. Safely up it, I turned,
Popeyed with fright, soaked and streaming.

They were *roaring* laughter. Jack's just
Drained face was reddening, split in laughing.
Irv slapped his thighs. "Hah! Hah! Hah-hah-
Hah! Hah! I don't believe it!" "Are you
Alright?" Norvel called. "Yeah, yeah,
I'm alright." Shocked, ridiculous, I
Joined them, bending over, body flushing and
Eyes tearing, insides quaking. Norvel dropped
To his side on the rocks, Jerry to one knee,
Jack turned half a circle, and Irv slapped
His thighs. "Hah!-hah!-hah! You—you
Look just like a drowned rat!"
It must've been ten minutes we laughed.

I pulled Norvel across. Getting off the branch,
He laughed. "Aren't you cold?" I changed
Out of hickory shirt and T-shirt into
Mackinaw and rain coat. Irv came last,
After the coils. We laughed in fits and starts.
Only Jack didn't ask if I was cold. We still
Had to lay out a new tail-hold. Irv gave me
The lightest coil. Drenched jeans (I didn't
Wear rigging pants with suspenders) clung
Against my heated legs. We climbed an earthen
Slide, outward steps pushing, calks digging,
Then through undergrowth and trees, our
Walks much shorter between stops. At one
Jerry said, "You should have seen

Jack's face. He went white as a sheet."
"Yeah, he turned white," Norvel said.
"He would've let you go up and sit in the
Crummie if you'd asked him," Jerry also said.
"No, I really feel pretty good," I said,
Satisfied in pride. I was good at packing
Coils uphill. I drew ahead. Jack appeared.
We went sidehill, switchbacking through the
Timber and its chilly shade. Laboring
Breaths puffed. Near the tail-hold hemlocks
We dropped coils about a hundred feet apart.
I took the last two more often and farther
Than anybody else, knowing even then
This pride was killing.

We got back to our nosebags, across the
Creek and up the other side, about 3:00.
Norvel raced over logs ahead of everybody.
Finally we got to eat. Irv still laughed
At what he called "the ducking." "You
Looked just like a drowned rat." "Yeah,"
Norvel said, "you were one surprised
Son-of-a-bitch." Jack, smoking, looked,
Away, disdainful out of disaffection. My
Ungloved hands freezing, I said that now,
Not moving, I was cold.
   I'd lost,
   Cast off, the
   Amazing, momentous
   Chance for connection.

April 25, 1976
and
February 18, 1982

Careering

Raving outside Pete's and Fast Eddie's taverns on the
    block of the Y.M.C.A. downtown,
Crew cut whitened, head as if neckless, stubble
    grizzled, glaring blue eyes
"Straight"—squat and ball-shouldered and still
    like a mountaineer,
The only poet in town once published by magazines
    his peers most valued
Pushes longhairs. "Are you going to *fight*, mister?
    Who's goddamn man enough
Here to stand up and *fight*?" Rupp is wild! He bulls
    from one to the next hanging outside
Their taverns after the two in Fairhaven closed—
    to be turned into banks—like
A toy with springs burst out. "Slow down, for God's
    sake, Bob. Slow down," says one.

He won't! The night blurred, blasted, but grotesques
    not disremembered—
Back 'em down! "Are you going to stand up, mister,
    or *sit down?*"
Another, not ignoring Rupp from knowing him, holds
    him back. Tears shine in
The poet's eyes. "My God, my God!" Sigh quavering,
    Rupp can hardly breathe. He
Faces one more of them, hugs him, booming, "By God,
    I need some *men!*"
Stepping back, shining eyes hardened, he demands,
    "Who's man enough here to soldier for *Bob Rupp?*"
        What's this? He's crazy-drunk! But—
        Why? What's happened to him?
        At what cost, for what gain, this?
        What have I come on here? And what
        Can be done?

Over ten years earlier Rupp moved up to the
Northwest where famous writers died young. He
Peddled his "poesies" out, published, and stayed
A star on the hill into the late 1960s. Things
Turned for the worse. Lyrics would no longer *go*
(And Rupp bumped against his art's assessors).
On the pot, quoting stanzas memorized as a
Student, he strained. At gatherings the brogue he put
On, less sure, couldn't be so confident. Most
Rupp knocked at the young once of a parade in his
Classes, as their forward body fractured,
Frustrated bitterly by masses—"Fucking
Phony kids, anyway"—
      Things at large work effects entire.
By '73 he and his third wife, her bones fine
To the short-bodied son of a Midwest dentist,
Had separated. He had an apartment
In a new Village, mixing whiskey and bloody
Marys with consoling a friend who *knew* she
Was dying of cancer. The publisher who had
Contracted for Rupp's third book wasn't going
Through with it. Strangers sometimes came up to the
Poet so amazing the night before.
Attacking the house that held his wife—knowing she
Was with some young stud in there—after closing-time
Again got him locked up. Cops and his P.O.
Couldn't *believe* the money a professor—
"Of poesy, for God's sake!"—made. Anti-abuse pill
Swallowed every morning, he served a
Dry year. The divorce went through. The last time
I saw Rupp, the July before this one, he
Was "holed up." "I didn't make this world, mister
... I don't ask anyone to come and tickle

My toes . . . I want to be alone."
          So he was, condensing a dimming,
          Compact with blooms that had shattered,
          Split, faded and hid.

Now!
          Beat, beat, beat against this crashing,
          Sinking night! To beat and still to beat—
          No!—bounce, bounce, bounce! But is even
          Faith in the poison lost? No!—to be a
          Victim-hero, fool-saint, slain for your art!
          Clown! Why not?—Summer term 's the dullest.
          But a man, still! Spew it back? Force *it*—
          Them—ah, who the hell know?—down, down, . . .
He sees me. Rupp's face opens incredulously.
"My son!" Rushing forward, he hugs me. "My son,
My son!"—his whitened head pressed to my
Shoulder, voice with a grateful sob, as if at
Deliverance from wilderness. "Where the hell did
You come from?" The book sold! This he has to tell
Immediately. "The goddamn, old, stuffed thing
Sold! They're gonna mount the bird! December. 'Tis
The season!" But he's lost his old Econoline.
"You remember the blue slug?" Left it somewhere
On the South Side. Never mind. "Come on. We'll go in
Here. What? Somebody pay this goddamn taxi
Driver! I'm in charge here!" The owner, come back to
Our table, knows Rupp. We're served. Talk of his
Book, others', friends and places disconnected, as an
Act sings the blues. Suddenly Rupp bolts up. "I'm
Getting out! Out *there*—out there is where the beauty
Is! Fucking beauty." He plunges for the door. Air!

On the sidewalk he confronts another longhair,

Demands, "Are you *a man? Are* you man enough
To come up against *Bob Rupp?*" This guy just stares. The
Poet's head bows. His head bent to his chest in
Solemn penitence—unwitting theater—Rupp
Sighs again. God is on all flaws. The man drops
To his knees, caught by hands, lunges to kiss a longhair's
Boots, does kiss concrete—The earth!—and heaves skyward,
Gaping—oh, to be a perfect fool, in glory
Through tribute!—and lunges next to kiss a collie.

Aghast, I watch, too stunned to comprehend this turn.
    Is this falling humiliation to become saint,
    Or is shame no longer shame in passing honor,
    Or is this for guilt from which he can create,
    Or is it but a sheering, thicker blotting?
Some help him stand. We hunt his Econoline,
Then I let Rupp out in front of the new taverns.
    Only later did I think that he,
    So carrying our times,
    Couldn't help—oh, he couldn't stop
    That breaking down.

September 15, 1976
and
March 11, 1982

Coming Down on the Ferry

Inside the Reclining Lounge
Foot-passengers rest in high-backed blue rows,
Suitcases, sleeping bags, backpacks beside them,
Or wander,

Hands with beards under caps, Tavern names
        on windbreakers, and
Women also "going Outside" from Alaska.
They'll be on at least the day and a night.
The Malaspina rides like a plated white cake,
Engines thrumming through its Decks. Evergreen
Islands edge straits, then a southward expanse.
Circling gulls dive to the wide, even wake,
Swoop by idlers along rails. This sunshine is
Lucky for October. The air cools. I return to reading.

Evening darkens seried windows,
Kid still playing with cutouts, coloring and tumbling
        across the carpeted front,
The three with plump, fair but rosy faces like
        Zee Paper's pastel tots
Watched by their mother, her smile theirs in dimpling.
Food tops her box. A homesteader near Hoonah, she'll
        be in Sedro Wooley a month before her husband.
The more able acrobats belong to a longhaired couple.
Their dad, his blond forelock receded,
Takes up guitars again with an Ivan.
"Love is like a fire," they sing,
"It burns you when it's hot ... " I go over,
Kids join "Yellow Submarine" and "Act Naturally",
Then voices stop and I cross back.

Lights out. Riders come up from the bar,
I swallow nips of Ten High, engines' "bump-bump-bump"
Through plates thrums a lulling constancy, and for me
In this recess that's yet of going on, Election Day
For an unwatched campaign near, the charge and
Despairing haunt,
"Do something, do something—For what, for what?"

Somehow presses less.

March 7, 1982
First version 11/'76

Another Somewhere of
Old Home Isn't

Places changed since I was a boy in them
Tear especially. Up the Britton Road
From Lake Whatcom a new asphalt road
Lies into bushy country of grass and evergreens.
Along one graded shoulder
String thin yellow pipes for electricity.

I trot up the curve, past a short,
Smooth black arm with topping Circle,
Farther than I'd expected. "Can it go to the other
Side?" I wonder, meaning the Mount Baker Highway
    that slants, out of sight, over a mile away.

Straight the asphalt lines between firs
Bluff like palisades, a Realtors sign nailed
In one lot being cleared. Past a crossing the pavement
Becomes packed, wet ground, bending but
Extending still. "The fuckers," I breathe.

It ends in a T. I trot left, toward the
Lake and Silver Beach, the grade school
I haven't seen in years, this
Dusking afternoon of Christmas Eve.
Soon more asphalt intersects, a street
Already residential, split-levels landscaped,
In the development for some reason titled
Tweed Twenty.

I cross, step up between jeep-wide tracks,
Angle through "the Woods" quiet but not so
Large as memory, toward the school, sidestepping
Puddles and cycle-treads. Where will *this* go?
Not far along, it seems, the wide trail forks,
And I take the right. Entered on a slight road,
Grass between its graveled ruts, I look back and
See, tucked behind terraced lawns and water wheels,
A white house—
The Mink Farm!—behind Big Rock pond—*far*
Beyond the school toward "town."
"This is Big Rock. This is behind Big Rock.
Isn't it?" I whisper.

March 7, 1982
First version 12/'76

A Bat

The afternoon a bat
Flew up in my hotel room
Skewing above the bed as if out of a pocket,
Dark, my hand's length but larger than in Life,
Weird wings flapping it *at* me—
      Springing stigmata from 'BLOOD' galore—
Ineffably unexpected—God, what a terror!

"A bat!"
Out I bolted,
Hunched and bristled, to the main hall.
"A goddamn bat! Jesus, what's a bat doing here?"
Late Sunday afternoon
I'm putting away things for writing,
Done, in my cramped but spruce room
Of an immaculate though unfrequented (three
Tenants and over 30 rooms) Scandinavian
Hotel in Ann Arbor, Michigan, December
Ice jagged across the window,
And a bat flies up?
      Real? Hallucination? Or sign?

I opened the door.
No bat.
Then—ah!—there
It stood, next to the nearest leg of my bed,
Low, mammalian with wings folded, drab
Brown and looking old—
      Like a beadle vested to chastise—
Relieving but again terrifying me.
What to do?
I pushed the door. The door swung back.
Twice more it did,

Aggravating, before the bat flew up
And I jumped back.
It flapped to the far corner,
To the doorway, and round again.
As it circled, wheeling level, wings
Noiseless and nodal nose ominously out, I
Stepped ahead, stayed the door with a chair.
            How was it here? Why?
I stepped toward the window. Suddenly—I
Twisted—the bat dove behind the lacquered dresser,
Skittering in its descent.
            Why had it done that?
Stillness. I proceeded,
Raising the window.
Space between it and a screen and above was
Enough for the bat to have come through when
The window was open earlier.
That seemed unlikely.
No phantom, nor visionlike "'Ah, Sun-flower!...'"
            Was the bat a test
            For me to be kind to it?
            Presented close to Christmas?

It walked out from under the bed.
I huddled backward.
It took wing, flapped in circles near the
Ceiling more.
            Why *wouldn't* it go out the door?
"Get out of here."
            Did it somehow sense, banking before the
            Open way, this room was its home?
It veered toward me. I shot up an arm. "Get
Out of here, goddamn it."
            With what to shoo it—
            But not *hit* it?

The bat landed next to my pillow,
Stalked with its wings folded, and *touched* my pillow.
        That was enough!
I rushed, outraged past thinking conscience,
Yanked the pillow: the bat took off: and
I swung and hit it.
It dropped.
Face down on the hardwood beside my desk,
The bat lay,
Still, stiff, littler now in its crumpling.
        Had I hit it so hard? With a pillow?
        It *must* be alright.
It moved. As I stared it at last
Scraped from wing to wing,
Small and brown and looking old,
Like a mole and like a toad,
Jerking against nature to right itself.
I lifted the screen. "I need something to
Prop this with." Thesaurus upright worked.
"That's where you're going, Joe."
But the bat could only scrape, jerking,
And I was still afraid to touch it.

Its thrusts grew sharper. Then,
Abruptly as before, it flew!
Returned to itself, *renewed*—
But back to circling it went.
"Ack," I sighed, exasperation affected,
"Get out of here."
And it did,
Flapping through the doorway, down the side hall,
Disappearing in a glimpse of its tail,
Though still in the hotel.

"Frankly, I'm glad it went,'
I said into the vacuum of fear and wonder left.

>Egoistically extending thought—humans'
Alone!—made of the weird visiting
A test—one grotesque, at that—from God.
I failed to see
The bat as a part of me,
Reason enough to be kind.

March 10, 1982
First version 12/'76

Colors Changed Color

Bayous, patches, and the Crescent, land lies low,
White tombs memorial over communities' Fields,
Plots legally not half a man's arm deep,
Bloodshed quick, air inspiratory with heat,
Where graves slip into water changing color.

"Lou-eez-ee-an-a!"
   Platform-rigs check the Gulf in fields of Blocks,
Always lighted,
Plumes of flame "flaring" gas.
   Come May, Cajuns can shrimp past three miles
Offshore. "Be-foh" the shrimp and crawfish run
"Coonasses" trap muskrats and nutrias and hunt
Frogs. Once, a man could make big money doing that.
   One Guillote, captain of a Company's tug,
Trapped on his seven days off for cash to keep his
Kids eating. "Morgan City used to have a good name."

Now he lived in a trailer camp up the Atchafalaya.
   Southwest, along Highway 90, by the Intracoastal
Waterway, thousands park in the yards of Companies
Building ships and rigs, platforms on their sides with
Legs consecutively canted like dark steel spars of
Fantastic armada.
   Cranes hoist pipe, cement, "mud" treatments,
Marine toilets and heaps of rusty scrap. Oyster
Shells serve like gravel on shoulders. The live
Oak grows out of supple and still fertile earth.
   Farther down, by old Jean Laffite's hideaway,
Land-rigs drilling beside rows of broken-stalked
Cane, sugar and sulfur factories, contrast
More with the fishing people's sleek new boats.
   While, from itty-bitty Kaplan to broad
Canal, the same kind of come-quick
Thing—neon gauds for Burger King et al.—
Sticks, to me, like a wrecker's ball
Burst, hanging, through one chaste white wall
Of a Hotel's court along Royale (1974).

These things, put on,
Don't really belong, you'll hear.
But the money's good,
And almost any man can make it.

Violence goes with the living,
The weather, even—oh, it shifts quick.
Corruption too 's always had open season.
"There are no laws around here,"
One vice-president of a drilling company advised,
Disparaging. The skipper of a crew-boat, who
Also lived away from Morgan City, said, "There
Are no commitments in Louisiana."

Out of Lounges tempers loosed cut and
Shoot. "Man, I was too *hot* t' think." Kindred
Abandon runs Trans-Ams off roads flat as your belt,
Cars rolling on tract-house lawns, sinking under
Bridges, decals and ruffles soaking blood.
        Making the news becomes the news.
In Rivers' Parish papers Tires Slashed and
Cows Shot hit boldly by politicians, their
Names a European roster, indicted for recent
Occasions to defraud, as in New Orleans last
Night's Crime warrants a register.
        The poor are robbed and maimed.
Amidst all this men of crossed races call
Each other "Sugar" and "Babe", expressions
Everyday but inherently easing, like the warmth
In natives' homes living beyond tradition.

We'd just come in from our "hitch" offshore,
Driving up from Grand Isle toward 90 beside
Rigs and cane and boats that still had a shine,
When Jack Groves, my driller, said, "You know,
Children and grandparents of these Cajun people can't
Talk to each other. They speak different languages."

        What was its own fertility—flashing—
        Turns like the lurid glare
        Of water under oil.

                              March 12, 1982
                              First version 4/'77

The Living Must Create

Now, what would Shakespeare do?
I often ask.

Neon-smiling boxes
Slide billions burgers to Hondas,
Renaults, streetwalkers (' "I'm hooked!" ').
More abstract,
Life is loops stranded? Or postulates unfreed?
Plasmid chimeras to be trustier beings from G.E.?
Or quark colors confined yet unfound in infrared
Slavery? "Philadelphia Freedom"?
Coke's jingle crosses into Top 40, Kiss is a
Hit in Tokyo too, Carter after Kissinger tends . . .
' "Then Starsky and Hutch stalk a vampire." '

This is some of the stuff
At which I shake,
Thrown less by it, though,
Than by how poor and dull we sit,
Our outrageous fortune a few's rule.

       Cried aloud in pain, fury and dread,
       He would have, I imagine, then, bearing
       Follies and woes as his humors could, gone
       On with what he had to do. Mighty Will!
       All as they can, but the living *must* create.

               March 12, 1982
               First version 5/'77

Over Dinner

See the car, see
Oil, put on, universal—
Taxis wait by sand-skirted curbs outside the
Swinging doors, Dar es Salaam—
See rice and beans
For dinner round the poor world.
    Won't the future
    Wonder how such
    Empire was engineered?

            March 12, 1982
            First version 7/'77

Kerosene Lamp

    Throw out
    Clichés of ours.
A kerosene lamp, Indian, flames by a tail of twine,
The register and book of receipts on a table in the
Iron-roofed Nyati and Simba Guest House, Ngorongoro.
    Burning for industry?
    Light of liberty?
"Nyerere", the old man who speaks falsetto—
Swahili worrying exclamatorily!—because gored by a
Buffalo, boils milk in a worn pot over charcoal
Wood-chips for "his" tea, as the boy, the lodgings'
Director, finished school, writes tourists receipts.
    Something new for us
    Is working up here.

            March 12, 1982
            First version 8/'77

By the Hand

I was so alien and lonely. Another Saturday night—
"Another Sad'day night, and I sure ain't got nobody"—in
Dar es Salaam, and I was obliged to go out to a 'Ball' for
graduates of the University. I had to see it to find out
more.

Six weeks into Tanzania, I was underfed and tired. Gas
from water swallowed swimming laps in the Mission to
Seamen pool bubbled in my stomach. My work-boots
rested on the cement floor of my room in the Zanzibar
Hotel as I lay on its bed. I heard Sam Cooke's song from
fifteen years before, when I was a boy. African Rock
repeated on the jukebox to a drinking crowd in the bar
below.

"Do you know where the New Mlimani Park Bar is?" I
asked Blacks and Indians standing outside a Fish and
Chips restaurant nearby. "New Mlimani?" One took me
into the kitchen. He translated an aproned Black's Swahili.
"It's out close by the University." A taxi that far would be
forty bob. Forty shillings—about $5.00! What about a bus,
and where? Yes, I could get one, but an Indian said that at
night the bus-stop by the old Post Office was "Dangerous."

I jogged toward it. Kabobs cooked smokily over iron
boxes on a corner of the roundabout where slanting
streets met. Provisions Store and Cold Drink Shop doors
were closed. Water dripped from balconies of cement
Mansions to sand in sewery gutters. Even Independence
Avenue, wider, lighter, where tourists shopped, was
desolate. Along City Drive a few Usafiri buses, stained by
exhaust, waited. Behind shaded outlines of palm trees on
the beach were dhows and anchored freighters. I asked a
neatly dressed Black which bus for the University and
then moved away, nearer a streetlight, apart from others
scattered in the dark.

After directing me to a bus that was stopping, the

stranger in a Slim Fit shirt took the seat for one ahead of mine. The bus lumbered out. Its condutor in khaki walked back with his belted change-box and tape of tickets. He waved away my shilling. The one ahead had paid my fare!

Amazed, I thanked him. He refused a shilling. I related that I'd been warned the bus-stop was "Dangerous." The bus wound through angling and sinuous streets, away from the close rows of downtown. We traveled a road. The stranger sitting ahead named larger, newer buildings between iron-roofed huts. He was studying Engineering. He struggled with English. Silences between us discomforted him. My sore eyes closed in woozy fatigue. At a crossroads the one who had helped me stepped out after telling me where to get off. "You are about five miles from the University here." "*Asante.*" My first suspicions shamed me.

The bus progressed. I moved forward and asked the conductor and driver, to be sure where I should get off. They seemed to not understand. Another young Black—all riding now were black—indicated that he knew my stop. Across his tight singlet was stenciled Bruce Lee/King of Kung Fu.

He motioned for me to stand up. We stepped out. "This is it?" I asked. Along either side of the tarmac was nothing but flat darkness. Buildings lighted on a hill appeared far-off. "Yes, the University," this Black said. He advised me to call a taxi from a phone up the road. How much to the New Mlimani? I asked. Oh, ten shillings. And how much in distance? "No," I said, "no, I'd rather walk, if it's only a kilometer, a kilometer and a half."

We followed women bearing bundles across the road and down another of tarmac, narrower, two lanes unmarked, into deeper darkness. Again I feared robbery. I also thought that the sinewy slim one now leading me

might be homosexual. He walked with a strut. A Black in
Western coat and trousers kept ahead of us.

"P'sst!" whistled into my ear. I jumped, arms snapping
up. "I know that man!" my guide said. A car had stopped.

We ran, the Black in a suit coat too. He sat in the front
of the Peugeot. All of them talked in Swahili. We went
through a crossroad. At least two kilometers passed by.
Moonlit fields of maize were all that was around us now. I
worried more that I'd been "set up."

The car stopped. Their voices intensified in argument.
Then the driver turned his Peugeot around.

He dropped us up the road we'd passed. Back of an
earthen parking-lot sat a low and wide cement building.
Blacks leaning against cars drank brown bottles of beer.
We all got out, thanking him. "Asante." "Asante."

We leaped a gully. "Just go with me." The one in
stenciled singlet, waiting, took my hand. I let him.

The New Mlimani Park Bar resembled someplace rural
where dances were held in the United States. Soldiers
stood by the door. My guide talked with one and then
urged me inside. We got in free. 20/- was the admission
advertised. I was amazed once more.

He pulled me along. Dancers crowded under dotting
lights stepped back and forth to local, metallic Rock
played by a band in back. We walked along a line of metal
tables also filled. At one, men sitting in simple shirts and
trousers greeted him. They talked. Two stood up and I
shook hands with them.

His and their parting tones sounding as if he promised
to come back, we shifted away. His unsweating hand still
held mine. "Those are my friends," he said. "Would you
like something to drink?" I gave him one or two 20/-
notes.

He squeezed into thronging toward a counter before the
front wall. The band went on. Its Rock was like reggae but

more percussive, steely and lilting. Couples danced as if walking in place while shaking tambourines. Dotting lights were strung like streamers from a hub over the floor. Smoke diffused congruously. Indians were infrequent and I saw only two Whites, tall, a couple. I knew no one here. My insides swelled and pitched with gas.

The helpful one brought bottles of Kiliminjaro beer. "Do they have ginger ale?" I asked. "You would like some ginger ale?" "Yeah, I would if—. No, wait—." But he'd already turned back toward the crush at the counter.

Somebody bumped me. I jerked round. A Black swayed, catching his balance unsteadily, in front of me. He was stout and drunk and wore a short-sleeve shirt. His eyes realized that I was white. "Hey, what you think about this?" he said. "What you think about comin' out here, mon?" "It's a lot like bars downtown, but bigger." "What you think about comin' out here, mon?" He thrust his head and cocked it at me. I glared. He took hold of my arm above the elbow with his free hand. I jerked loose and turned toward the dancers. He held my arm again. "Yeah, what you think—." I spun at him. "Look, I don't know you and I want you to leave me alone." We faced each other.

The one helping me appeared. He pushed and spoke sharply to the drunken Black.

"He doesn't know anything. He doesn't understand. He's drunk. Come. Come, we can sit down away from here." "Good, good," I said. He had a bottle of ginger ale.

Taking my hand, he led us forward along the near side, down an aisle between tables. Beer was spilled on metal tops and the cement floor. Blacks sat smiling and some lurched alongside us. We stopped by a table for two. Next to it a couple were opposite a longer table.

He indicated a lone chair, its seat and back plastic. I protested, but he stood a carrier on end for himself.

As we sat I could see him more closely. He was lean but
delicately made. Muscles in each of his arms were like a
single sinew. His waist was thin. The skin of his face was
tight like a drumhead. His cheekbones were prominent.
His eyes flicked alertly. I still wondered if he was
homosexual. Regularly I saw Blacks holding hands
downtown, but I never knew if this was simple friendship
or they were lovers.

"Do you come out here a lot?" I asked.

"Yes, quite often. I live near here," he said.

'You seem to—know quite a few people."

Yes. Some of the men at the table worked with him.
What did he do? He worked "in the spare parts shop"; it
was for vehicles of the University. For long? Five years.
Silence, then I said, "What a lucky night" and told about
the other Black helping me—paying my fare!—and the
forewarning.

"I heard you asking on the bus. You see, when a white
man talks like, "Here, boy"—then, no, we will not listen,"
my benefactor shook his head sharply. "But if he asks,
like you were doing, then we will help." "Uh-huh." Silence.

"Yes, very lucky. If your friend hadn't picked us up we'd
still be walking," I said, prosily forcing humor. He burst
into laughter. He was very nervous.

He wasn't from Dar es Salaam, was he? No, from
Bukoba—he could see Lake Victoria from his house there.
He came here seven years ago, living downtown before he
found the work that he had now. "Some of the men you
met live with me."

"Uh-huh," I said. "Close by?" "Yes—just along the road."

The band—The Workers' Band, I remembered from the
ad—had gone on break. I asked his name. "Kiisa?"
"Kiiza," he said with more vibrato. I spelled it. "Yes," he
nodded.

"I'm sorry for being so dead. If there's anything you want

to do, don't worry about me." *No, no,"* he shook his head.
"It's *you* who shouldn't worry—you shouldn't worry about
me." I smiled. I'd drained the ginger ale with desperation,
but my stomach still was hurtfully heaving. We looked at
our bottles of beer.

"I'm going to visit my friends before they leave," he said,
"but I'll be back." "Okay. Good. If I'm not around when you
come back, I will just have taken a taxi." He halted,
correcting me in alarm. "Oh, you *shouldn't* take a taxi. Too
much. You can stay with me. It's near here."

"Well, there's some work I want to do in the morning.
We'll see."

"You can have a good rest before going home," he said.
"But you do what is best for yourself."

"Okay. Thank you."

I shut my eyes when he was gone. The gas had but little
ebbed. I drank again and deliberately burped, then
moaned. The seas that were sore in my stomach would
not cease. And with them was my disorienting loneliness.

> Stay with him?
> I thought of Rimbaud's lover in Africa,
> The Arab boy
> Who'd taken care of him,
> Whom he'd called to see before dying.
> *Stay* with this "Kiiza",
> Nervously helpful, sinewily slender, this
> Native—and
> Find out more against my fears?
> A "good rest"? Yes, it
> Might be best—to
> Even sleep in his arms.

A woman with straight-cut khanga cloths folded round
her picked up bottles, piled them in a carrier. Kiiza

returned. He sat in the chair I'd moved over. "I had to be gone longer than I expected," he said. "Are you feeling better?"

"Nope," I said. "No, a little."

"Perhaps you want to go home?" "No. No, I'd like to hear more of the band."

As we waited I asked him about Nyerere, Tanzania's President, and if he thought much of the idea, the principle, of *ujamaa* in his daily living. The tradition of ujamaa in villages of this country was promoted by the government to be cooperation as if the entire nation was an extended family. Looking down, Kiiza said, "Yes, I think of it," then faced me. "You see, it's good that I should know you and that you should know me."

When the Workers' Band stepped back to their poised instruments I wanted to move closer. Kiiza led us next to the board-floored platform.

Jostling among young Blacks crowding forward tipped over the singer's mike-stand in the beginning of the next set. His Swahili berated them angrily. Police pushed them back. My eyes closed. Fatigue, the crowding, repetition, noise and my isolation.

The next song started. I said, "I'd like to go."

"You'd like to go home now?" Kiiza asked outside the 'Ball.' There were people approaching and taxis still. "I'd like to go to sleep," I said to prompt him. "I'm really tired."

"You'd like to have a rest before you go to your hotel?" "Yeah, I would." He lifted his head, agreeing as if he hadn't invited me.

We walked into darkening up the road of packed dirt that Kiiza's friend had first passed. Two boys in loose shirts and trousers walked the other way. Winking fireflies dotted among shaded, drooping leaves of maize. Frogs were in chorus. I said this sounded like fields where I was raised. Kiiza was unsure where the Pacific Northwest was, but knew Canada and particularly Vancouver. "Bar-rocq, bar-rocq," I echoed the frogs. Kiiza didn't imitate them.

He turned onto an entryway of softer dirt. It forked around two consecutive, smooth cement buildings that were like military housing. Behind them palms overtopped other trees. "This is where you live?" Upright in his walk, Kiiza nodded.

On the back side of the front building he knocked at a door marked K-8. Rustling inside. Opening the door wide as her head was a woman in darkly bright khanga prints. Kiiza spoke Swahili to her explanatorily. Her full, rounded face peered just after waking. She nodded but questioned. He gestured for me to wait and stepped inside.

Come back, he said. "You can sleep in my room."

He opened an adjacent door, undesignated and unlocked, to an ending room of the short block. Frame and box spring leaned next to a closet. A couch, too. I said I could sleep on it. "No, it is our custom," Kiiza said. "Please sit down." He dragged a mattress from next door. We set up a bed and put linen on it. Twice I replied that I didn't use a pillow, when he offered one. "I'm sorry, if you're used to having a blanket," Kiiza said. "No, just sheets. Too hot for more."

He sat in a cushioned chair before the table and I on the couch. We felt we should talk. "Do you sleep here?" Kiiza shook his head alertly. "No, this is my—study," he said with a hesitation. "I come here to be alone." I nodded without understanding his relation to the men who "lived" with him and to the woman next door. While he'd been gone for the mattress I'd looked about the room. Aside from the couch of red cushions and scratched arms and the chair before the low table, there was a desk against the back wall, a bare wooden chair at it. A bookcase with books on engineering and athletics. And on walls sheeted by fiberboard were postcards of zebras, elephants and highland forest, along with magazine photographs of black, white and Oriental women. The room, seeming bare but cramped, sought brightening and substantiality from within and outside Tanzania.

I was too tired to ask more. The sore swells and pitches in my belly had quieted. "Well, thank you. I can't say asantes, thank you, enough." "You want to go to sleep," Kiiza said.

I fell to rest like timber, grateful for his generosity.

Sounds of washing woke me. Outside the door a baby in diapers stood on concrete with its knees fleshily dimpled, sucking a wedge of orange.

Inside a room for washing at the near end of the walk the woman from next door was bent over a sink beside a curtained, metal shower-stall, khangas wrapped across her back." *Jambo,* "I greeted her. "Jambo," she said. "Kiiza is not up yet." The sun already rose starkly through palm and fig trees behind the housing opposite.

Kiiza soon knocked. "Are you feeling better?" he asked. "Oh yeah—a lot," I said. "Just what I needed."

That morning I found out the woman was his wife. The baby, their son, was two years old. At my referring to books in the case he said that he played football (soccer) and told me about the team that he and other workers in the spare parts shop had. We dropped into silences again.

I couldn't stay for breakfast—I wanted to go right to work—and he and his wife couldn't have breakfast with me downtown—because they had their baby. "It would be awkward for us this morning."

Later, we agreed, exchanging names and addresses. Kiiza, barefoot and bare-chested when he came in, splashed himself with water, re-entered in his singlet stenciled with Bruce Lee/ ... He would "escort" me to the bus.

One of his friends at the table the night before now sat

on the opposite walk. We waved. So that was how they lived together, I thought. Children skipped in front of a naked baby sucking fruit.

Kiiza and I waited by a pole with KITUO on its topping disk. Across the road a small truck delivered buckets of sail-shaped green and white liters of milk. Natives also went to and from the porch of the store out here. On the hill multi-story buildings of the University stood out, more brilliant but flatter under sunshine. It wasn't yet 7:00. Kiiza looked off, uneasy that we still forced talk or were silent. Saying that I would call, I ran for the bus with relief.

We met "for a swim" the next Sunday. Only when he got to my room did Kiiza tell me that he couldn't swim. "But you shouldn't worry. I'll enjoy myself." Breezeless air downtown was like a broiling oven. We walked out, forgoing the bus, past sewery ditches alongside broken sidewalk and then gardens of embassies, to Oyster Bay. While Kiiza waded I swam. Two Blacks also rode the breakers. In unspoken challenge we stroked out toward a chain of anchored freighters waiting for the harbor, bobbing against the waves, swallowing salt water, glimpses gaping at each other, till we all floundered. When we'd stumbled up to shore they told me that they'd been swimming for just a year. "We didn't want to turn back before you." "Well. Well, we needed more communication, more communication out there." They were from Bukoba too. One drove a truck and his friend studied accounting in Dar es Salaam. Kiiza said he didn't know "those boys from Bukoba"—over a thousand miles inland. They practiced Kung Fu moves on each other. We sprinted aong the beach.

We walked back, showered in the hotel, and for dinner ate *ngali,* beef upon warm, ground maize that's thick as porridge, in a bar and restaurant I'd found. Silences often

occurred between us, still, but that day with Kiiza I felt an
ease, a tranquility, I'd seldom known. We parted by the
angling street, close with Mansions, where he would catch
a bus out to his home.

I didn't see him again. The next Saturday I flew out. I
didn't get to his team's practice Thursday and mesages left
at the spare parts shop and the Zanzibar's "desk" never
got through. By Saturday noon we just had time to say
good-by over the phone.

> What of our meeting, then?
> Against my suspicious fears
> Kiiza showed a little more
> Of the giving that was there.

February 6, 1982
First version 9/'77

Chipping and Painting

Head to the job
"Rack-ack-ack-at-at!: Rack-ack-at-at-at!: . . . "
—The needle- and scraper-guns hands hold,
Vibrating from compressed air through hoses,
Pepper old paint, cut scale of rust,
Beat to Decks and Rooms of the tender-ship
Docked at Bethlehem in Beaumont.
And: "Whang!"—
With chipping-hammer you
Smite iron more,
Knocking off coating and crust,
Before you can brush on an -ene
And paint it.

> Recall "Wishin' And Hopin' "
> Sung by Dusty Springfield,
> Among the Pop songs and variations that
> May play along with doggerel:
> "Just chippin'/And paintin'/
> And paintin'/And chippin'/ . . . "
> Yeah, you need to get a set,
> Need a little humor to forget
> What you're doing, where you are.

Downtown Beaumont stands behind corrugated Shops
of the Bethlehem Shipbuilding Yard. Drab buildings
there have been left in the flight from ingrown
poverty. The river along the Yard and Docks is
browned too. Pines on an island flake. Platforms aban-
doned on it stick legs out. Behind this brushy knoll
in late afternoon traffic (cars, pickups, semis)
jams a bridge of I-10. At night lights spaced in
front of Shops shimmer like pointing pools of solder.

And then the water when smooth may reflect glistening
like oil.

We're fed well. Three sit-down meals a day: on
Thursdays and Saturdays there's steak for supper,
when Crews come in after 6:00 from our supposed
12-hour "tower": and at least once a week Coonass
cooks' dark, green-laden, shrimp-succulent gumbo.

Since September this old drill-ship 's had men
converting it here. December 15th was the last date
set for it and us to go offshore. We're into February
now. The day after New Year's Bruce, another rough-
neck, and I were patching on the Second Deck with
red lead. "We're not doing anything," he said.
"Yeah," I said. "Paint it up nice where they
can sink it," Bruce said.

It's just a write-off, we agreed.

5:00 every morning the siren
Gets up whatever two of the four (A,B,C,D)
Crews are on, hitches fourteen days long. We
Eat and go out to jobs: to
Roll pipe, sandblast walls and buoys, run
Wire, lay grating, cut and/or weld or watch
"Fire", check valves and check Pumps, wash
Pits and wash Decks,
Chip and/or paint—to, in short,
Work and/or "keep busy",
Or, hungover from a night out from four-bunk
Rooms, "hide."

      Trifling, trifling, trifling!
      Fractions (titled Roughneck, Roustabout,
      A.B., Welder, Electrician, . . .) in
      Paying oblivion,
      "Running on" and "Slip-sliding away",

We sense—as trash burns
Under the steam-powered crane—
We but waste.
Oh, that's toil's real toll,
These days of partnering iron and oil!

March 13, 1982
First version 3/'78

May 31, 1978

Driving the Nation Merged

"Na'Orlens" to "Nee Yawk"
Miles and miles of concrete
Interstates bind beside
MOTEL bulbs, Lounges, fuming plants,
Past shanties, to red earth
Flanking piney hills, M's,
Then A's toward smokestacks blowing
Over Bessemer, swelter
Lingering into the dark—
Inns of Knoxville irradiated right hand and
     left hand!—
And morning sunshine dawning to
Colonial fronts, more
Omelette Shoppes and Waffle
Houses in green Virginia,
Steady through hours rolling
To Pennsylvania
And its -burgs, plastic awnings
Of rows in from 78

Of the System shielding
Light like bills before brick stoops,
Townspeople splashing in
The pool by League baseball—
JOHNNY'S neon in malls with A & P and Winn-Dixie—
And into another
Night, arrived in the
End city, the same markets
Adjoin Agostini's.
I see—ten years after thumbing untrodden Turnpikes—
All that's on the country
Is done—
  Ah, all that's on
  This country is done, blanking
  Recognition!

Dullness

Why do I have nothing to say?
The absence—too dull for anguish—
Does worry me;
It feels like my time to twenty-seven and
The present
Together void inspiration.

Hills in Tennessee

Hills up toward Chattanooga, called mountains,
(Hey—'See Ruby Falls!')
Bristle dark green,
Trees blanketing, clumped or overhanging
In a long, long valley
Through rugged gaps that crook quickly.
  Their own still.

March 13, 1982
First version 5/'78

All under Stars

Times—oh, I remember
When we in the Silver Beach gang,
Grade-school and junior-high
Age, ran bare-ass naked in front
Of cars' (neighbors'?) headlights:
The tingling creep down, solo in
Shared dare, the scamper and
Scramble back into bag, laughter
Hitched by heartbeats.
Then, stares to the immense,
Sparkling night sky arched over all,
We saw strange lights flash or
Track, talked about the life sure from
There finding us.
Later (I was in high school),
Lying back from a girl as in a
Tumbling fall from heat reached,
I saw—she and you may have too—
Us dwarfed above.
Those years I also stalked
Mystic experience in boxer shorts,
Barefoot about dark banks
Of Broadway Park, squeezing/smelling needled
Humus—the earth!—between
Ducking headlights. Older though
Teen-aged still, I unrolled
A bag on States first-met, under
More hemispheres
And yet the same
Mysterious envelopment.
     Strange, how it's the wonder ' lasts!

March 14, 1982
First version 8/'78

Falling Star before MacArthur Drive

What? What have we done?
Hours into days, over hundreds of miles,
My brooding shock sits,
Incoherently dumb.

Bluey flaming ball
Darts like a rent
Down the night sky
And out—Poof!—before sign
For Exit to MacArthur Drive in Tracy
      ahead, along 580 West,
And suddenly
The horror I've
Carried through a trip to the Northwest and
Back at the murders and 'MASS SUICIDE'
By over nine hundred in their "Jonestown",
Guyana, that inert dark succeeded in Redding by
The radio's "In San Francisco this afternoon ex-
Supervisor . . . killed the mayor, . . .
And Supervisor . . . " and my
Unanswering shout, "What? What did he do?",
Lights up in awful coalescence.

      Look! Look at what we've done,
      All we've put on!
      No wonder they went with their drugged lord
      In despair, no
      Wonder the cracking!
The news had told more: offshore-oil leases granted,
The dollar to be strengthened, running claimed a
New religion . . .
And snapping symptoms shot together with the
Flaring of that star.
      Now is only the start.

51

March 14, 1982
First version 11/'78

Mid-Manhattan,
Drinks After Work

They sit
With glazes over their faces,
Man and man, women together, and man and woman
On high-legged chairs round the bar and in booths
Of this dusky Place
That offers Dixieland Jazz nights,
A sunny, hot afternoon, a weekday in June.

Men with lost hair,
Hunched by the bordering pad, suitcoats unbuttoned
Over their paunches,
Talk among themselves
Or to "ladies" not past twenty-two
Whose stances and eyes shift impatiently;
Pallor surrounds flushes in these men's faces,
While the hookers-like-teen-girls looked bored.
        How respite is wanted!
Women, jackets undone back on their shoulders,
Reach for pretzels at tables.
Not old, but no longer young,
They with nostrils glacé yet pinched
Glance about this dark space too,
As if hunting some spark
Between offices and apartments—
        Ah, homes of boxes!
Smoke from cigarettes just lit is quickly taken.
Around 5:30 hors d'oeuvres are served at a station.
Customers file. At the piano
Another waitress in saloon-girl's flounced black
Plinks rags by Joplin used in "The Sting."
        How respite is wanted
        From homes of boxes!

Here is no real retreat
From death-in-life,
From walled insanity.

March 15, 1982
First version 6/'78

Seeing Europe Lost

Beautiful,
Beautiful old places,
Creations, touches,
        And mad-made, spoiling things
On the continent where we rose with visions.

Postcard scenes! Alpine valleys,
Hillsides along the Rhine,
Their textures as by old masters:
Arbored strasses, swayed City Gates,
That stand yet with care for masses,
The vaults of Cathedrals to godly spaces,
The ideal of David besmirched but towering:
With acts for welfare—
        That wars most make common—
Accented by awe and dread of the American.

Such beauties,
Magnificence, and common acts to awaken
Are now shaded
By plants bigger than any Square or Castle,
Spread against forests and orchards,
Stars of Mercedes Benz and Fiat on smokestacks,

And SHELL, BP, ESSO along -bahns, Old roads, Vias,
By McDonald's displacing cafés beside cobblestones,
And most insidiously by Pop logos
Across unbordered fronts (Working For You).

>   Europe
>   Inescapably follows
>   The States at least feared;
>   Shades from the Eagle roost.

To see our past here taken
Tears, tears at the tourist's somehow rooted heart,
And to think what *may* be lost—
>   *Rembrandt*...with
>   The land and people—
Lays a dread like acid in the belly.

March 15, 1982
First version 6/'78

Holes in Blocks

In Projects raised
Beside freeways
Blocks of brick or
Concrete bunched,
Broken windows
Gape above black
Or colored scrawls.
>   The kept and rent
>   Wait for openings
>   Before they break out.

March 15, 1982
First version 10/'79

One with Junk!

On a Greyhound by the Waterway
Got an old rider by my side.

Out of New Orleans,
But close to Fat City,
Some strip loaded more than I remember,
Both sides of multilanes,
Stretches, unending, ahead.
Halloween evening, bulbs of
Christmas red and green
String as from a Maypole over Cars lots,
Neon of franchises and Bank branches
Glares more hazing,
Gas-station signboards present
$1.69 8-Pak Ponies and 89¢ Liters of pop
Between a Giant Supermarket, lots of Trailers, Auto
Parts, Records and Tapes, Scuba Diving and Sex Shops,
Godchaux's here apposed with Macy's in malls, and—
Whoa!—I mean: *Woe!*

Would you be one with it, Walt,
In this state where your genius was loosed?
Could *these* Shapes
Be dear to you?

In back seats—
Safer for drinking and smoking—
That smell of pop and gum,
Guys with Rock tours decaled on T-shirts
Over the low waists of their bellbottoms
Call each other dude. They may have seen each
Other before. They're going, like me, to some

Job offshore. They talk about firing up doobies,
Popping beers. " *Fuck* that driver." "We
Got to party tonight." Though: "There are fifteen
Dudes for every chick in Morgan City."
    They go on,
    Fed and feeding,
    Unending, it seems, as 7-11s
    Of the ghastly, devouring spread!

    For them the joyous clank, Walt?
    Will their labor hold them to God?
    Aw, come on now.
    To *not* be of such blight,
    Let the gods in us wake!

March 16, 1982
First version 11/'79

On Viewing Cockroaches
in the Northern and Southern United States

(Anywhere you see *many* cockroaches,
It's probable the bug not much bother you.)

This difference, still:
Happen on a roach,
Even some *monster* with a back like the Monitor,
Scurrying out of a sink in the South,
It more likely goes with the weather—
    And the sustaining through readiest chance—
There
Than up North,
Where a cockroach
Appearing in most homes
Cleared on colder, harder grounds
Can shock—
    Like an offense to the order won with God—
Yet.

March 16, 1982
First version 11/'79

Marsha's

Sticky-warm March Friday in New Orleans,
Near suppertime evening, got kids
Wheeling and chasing in their tennies along
The aslant sidewalk and up grated stairs,
Through the back door, got more, friends' and
Neighbors' and Marsha's girls, spread at cards

On the kitchen floor.
        Jeez, I think, stepping over,
        Is this how black people live?

Scouting out streetlit windows, between plants
Hanging and standing and walls of
Luteous (" *Beauteous*") Fall foliage,
Nikki (Nicole), eleven, the
Oldest, cries, "Momma's home! Momma's home!"
Danni ("*Danielle*," she'll tell you) hops
Out like a pixie. "Where? Where?" "No she ain't,"
Jason, the middle, corrects his
Sister. He's right, but— "Now she is." "Lem'me
See, lem'me see!" "Momma's home! Momma's home!"
They rush to clean the two bedrooms
Where all of the apartment sleep. Marsha
Climbs the front stairs. In her black boots,
Lacy shawl, white blouse and flower-strewn dark
"Hippie" skirt, her stature could be
A great athlete's. She sits on the couch, eyes
Like a tired, brooding lioness's,
After asking her "darling sugarpuddin's"
What they've done. They know not to press.

Saturday "C.C.", one brother, and a friend,
In from Biloxi, are sacked out
On chair and couch, kids and me in bedrooms,
When Marsha gets up to wash clothes
Before putting in the morning at Ronnie
The dentist's office, his handy lady.
Meals we eat in the front room too.
Sunday morning it's S.R.O., children
Running, bumping, swatting, spatting round their
"Granddaddy Joe" Cordier, as

Other "so-called adults" figure out who
Gets who and what this day. More than
Once Marsha says, "I *know* everybody
Else here is crazy."

    She holds scenes together, their energy
    Centers in her who calls friends "Boo",
    Who similarly tells her kids of their
    "One and only beautiful mother in the
        whole wide world",
    Apart out of pride,
    Like a plant herself,
    The strong and tender and most essential
        animal.

                March 17, 1982
                First version 4/'80

Fireflies in Pennsylvania

Winking about
Night-dark grass alongside I-80—
Like a sequin-network dotting randomly,
Like spectral electrons—
Electric in winking webwork in and o'er obscure,
    night-full grass
That beaming semi's blow past—
What?
Fireflies! Of course (their tails lights).
     Why in God's name are we here
     If not for wonder
     At such?

Thundershower over Cheyenne

Dark, bluff but outstretching
Clouds roll in fast from the West,
Pour big-dropped rain that
Damps June-dusty ground with a teasing smell.
Hard—and gone.

March 17, 1982
First versions 6/'80

God's Form

There's a God to test you,
But
He-or-She is in you
Now.

Spectacular Ruby Falls

Has anybody seen
Sweet Ruby Falls?
Or has that woman's love
Been taken to town again?

March 17, 1982

John Lennon Is Killed

Anguish,
Oh, helpless, helpless anguish,
After the fact,
As I walk,
Benumbed, breaths puffing to hold sorrow
    at the brims.
      WHY?
      Why has this happened? Why was he taken now?
But no why
Answers
Save the entire madness
We inhabit.

On a day not arousing, like most of late,
The news leaped at me from a newspaper-case—
FORMER BEATLE KILLED.

Details told more of woe to be wrung. A
Fan approached again as John and Yoko,
Back from recording, stepped out of their
Limousine in New York City.

"Mr. Lennon?" he asked. From learnt combat-stance
He fired five shots, three to the chest, and the
Star fell to pavement.

"Do you know what you've just done?"
"I've just shot John Lennon."

In a speeding squad car, its siren wailing
Off walls, Ono, huddled beside her mate
Like a mother bereaved, screamed, 'Tell me
It isn't true!"

An officer asked if he was his name,
But, bleeding, Lennon could only mumble
And moan.

The suspect, age twenty-five, a one-time
"Jesus freak" from Georgia, then Hawaii,
Also played the guitar.

Radio stations repeat songs
"In tribute to the legend of Lennon"
through the day and night.

What a voice—of voices—he had!
John the rock'n'roller—"Dizzy, dizzy
Miss Lizzy!": and balladeer—"Here I stand,
Head in hand ...": seer become sardonic—"Well,
I told you about the fool on the hill, ...":
And preacher—"*Im-ag-ine* all the people
Living in har-mon-ee/Aih'yee, h'h' ... "

Ah, John, John, John—Gone!

Like another Christ in Pop,
He was the victim of his heart.
More than that, though,
This shooting out of the dark
Means, I fear; it
Signs an end to hopes we've lost,
Another light forever
Down, murders of
Never before to break more
From the sore hollows in us.

But I hardly think,
Merely walk,
Puff-puff-puffing at news most sinking to the stomach,
Mourning the dear one lost,
And hearing his songs.

March 17, 1982
First version 12/'80

On the Floor

On the floor
"Iron" of pipes and "tongs"
Bangs, tightened chain
Rattles, cable screeches and
Behind "the drawworks" smoking
Diesel-electric motors
Rev.—
Noise and big things
Close around roughnecks' throwing,
Pulling, pushing ("Let's show some *snap!*)
And rests
In their jobs' enclosing synchrony.
On the floor
"Tripping pipe," move it fast;
Even when you're "making connections,"
Watch your fingers—"Watch your ass!"
On the floor
That so encloses (steel, planks,
Hanging tools and four-square
Legs of the derrick's "mast"),
"Coming out of the hole"
Or "Going in",
And even in the crew's
Easy time when drilling
Fills their "tower",
Working can get
Long, wearying, wearing;
Wearing beings brutally,
All close like beasts bound
To this working with iron for oil.

Offshore

In the Gulf
Both drill-crews' tower
Lasts twelve hours,
Noon to midnight or the other way
Splitting night and day
Between meals in the galley,
Sleep in bunks of quarters,
Below.
Through steel
Of rigs' legs,
Tubular and right-angled,
Rearing platforms and derricks of a Block
In the field surrounding,
Always lighted over water,
Dusks and dawns blur.

Tripping Pipe: Coming Out
of the Hole

"Takes teamwork, son!"
The three hands on the floor of a drilling-rig,
the derrick-man above them, and the driller facing
them at his controls alongside the drawworks, got
to bring the "stands" of pipe out together.
Say you're just starting.
The top stand in the string of drill-pipe rises
straight, a tubular train ascending from underground
through "the rotary table", lifted by "elevators"
toward the man on his "monkey-board" ninety or
so feet up in the derrick.
Two joints of the stand go by. When the bottom
shoulder of the third appears all floor-hands move
fast.

The chain-hand sets "the slips", throwing
or kicking their heavy taper off the lip of the
rotary table into *its* hole, the toothed dies in
the slips' mouth clenching the stand under an up-
sloped shoulder; the slips brace the entire string.

Just then the other hands, working "breakout"
and "makeup" tongs that hang in the derrick,
wrench jaws—already latched around the pipe—
of these tools. They jerk the grips lean *into*
the spoon-handle tail of tongs (over five feet
long), making dies in the jaws *bite* the steel
shoulders opposed over and under "the crack"
between joints.

Tight the strain draws as the driller turns
his knobs. Chain winding around "the breakout
cathead", a flanged shaft that extends from one
end of the drawworks, is drawn taut, knotted to
the tail of the breakout tongs. Tighter the
strain.

Pressure increases. Then the top shoulder that
hands watch turns. That's it! "It's broken."

The chain-hand unlatches tongs. The others
pull them back.

The stand unthreaded by the driller *pops* out
of the bottom shoulder.

One hand pushes it over to be planted in a
line on ring-rowed planks, the driller dropping
elevators—that the man overhead unlatches. He
above then hauls with a rope the top end of the
stand and lays it between "fingers."

As the driller sends the elevators, their now
open embrance hung from "the hook", one-and-a-
half-inch cable of stranded steel now spooling on
the drum of the drawworks, down fast as he wants.

The elevators, handled by two, are clapped under

the waiting shoulder.
   The slips are pulled.
   And the procedure repeats.
   So it goes ("Make those son-of-a-bitches
bite!" the driller may instruct) down to
"the drill-collars", each over twenty thousand pounds,
weightier pipe near the bit, when, kneeling and
hammering, you have to add "the clamps."
   And wash and scrape this pipe of spiral grooving
extra clean ("Knock that formation off 'a them
drill-collars!"), kneeling again, wet by water
from the hose some hand holds,
   As "mud", the cooling fluid pumped down and
up the string, may (raised to overflowing by
pressure below, mud may have spewed out when
joints were "broken", erupting like a geyser—
"Keep that mud-guard closed, goddamn it!"—and
thereby soaking hands brownly "nasty") also slick
the floor.
              And roughnecks might sing:
              "Slippin'/And a' slidin'/Reelin'/And a'
              Knockin'/Sloppin'/And a'..."/—"C'mon
              Everybody, let's do the Swim!/..."
The whole body, close and quick,
Heated and bonded by
Rhythms of mechanical but satisfying
Synergy when the working
Goes smooth, repeating tasks,
"Gets after it"
Down—as we *were* going—
To the bit
That Buddy or Roger or Ronnie or Bruce might pet.

: Going In

"Throwing the chain"
Is the key
Action for unison
This trip.
　　After a fresh bit, say, of teeth pointing
inward on three roller cones, the mouth like a
moray's, the teeth's length and hardness judged as
best to "make hole", is screwed on, and "the
sub" and drill-collars are also made up, the
chain-hand starts his denominative job.
　　Now things go in reverse.
　　Overhead, the derrick-man lays into elevators
the last stand of drill-pipe taken out. He claps
the elevators shut. And the driller hoists the
stand embraced.
　　Its bottom end *springs*, its lean leaping off
the ring impressed on wood. One hand's straight
arm slows the spring. He jumps with it, catching
it again, as the shivering steel still jerks at
the pipe held by slips in the hole. Hugging it
with one crooked arm, he—and maybe another—
"stab" this suspended stand into threads doped
inside the shoulder of the pipe waiting. Several
"wraps" of "spinning chain", set around the
lower shoulder, rest on latched makeup tongs.
　　Next, the flip.
　　From five or so feet away the chain-hand throws
the spinning chain, backhanded with his right nor-
mal, the braided-rope tail of the chain gripped
in his palm. This snaps a bow through the length
of links to the pipe, throwing the wraps clear
over the margin of threads spaced between shoulders
　　Just as the driller starts the top stand in.

The chain coils in a rattling spiral up the
top shoulder, turning tight, pulling the hand to
the uniting stands as its length winds off the
upper, shortening, rattling, taut, to "the makeup
cathead" back on the driller's side of the draw-
works. The hand might have to come to the coils,
cover their smoking under friction with his pebbled
cotton gloves, before the shoulders are flush and
this new crack squeaks.
   When that's done, it's enough. "It's tight."
   The tail flies off, back by the driller. The
tongs latched around the lower shoulder, acting
as back-up like any wrench, are pulled off, back,
and stopped by knot or hook away from the action.
   Slips are pulled.
   The train three joints longer drops with
elevators.
   And roughnecks get ready for the next stand
to go in.
> They might sing: "Oh, this trippin'/This
> Grippin'—and flippin'—and haulin'—and
> Fallin'—/Gets a body rippin'.
> But boss: Hour after hour, and tower
> After tower/With nothin' to
> Do in between/Got
> To wear the souls of old boys out."

Making Connections
(Making Hole)

"This is your ass-time. Enjoy it."
When drilling fills their tower
Roughnecks have plenty of rests.
   "Hole" is made by "the kelly", square-
sided and forty or so feet high, turning to the

right, twirling like a skater stroboscopic in
its bushing, focal on the floor now, above the
table and under the ingenious "swivel";

It and hundreds thousands pounds of weight
on the bit, governed by the driller, keep cones
rolling, teeth boring, below.

The string of pipe into the hole is lengthened
one joint at a time. For this hands come back in-
to action.

Once the kelly is spinning down near its top
above the bushing, another joint is needed. The
kelly is hoisted, broken from the last joint in,
pushed over to a joint poking out of "the mouse-
hole" between table and fronting "V-door". The
kelly and waiting joint are made up with chain
and tongs.

The extension is hoisted, hook higher, pushed
over, and the fresh joint is made up with the
last—the crack *tight*. Chain and tongs are taken
off. Slips are pulled. And that—the procedure
should be done in less than a minute from first
break on—'s a connection.

The kelly twirls downward again.

Hands attend to jobs. The driller watches his
gauges, works his clutch and brakes. The derrick-man
goes back to check pressures on his pumps and the
cuttings that circulating mud flows up from the
hole over vibrating "shakers". Floor-hands choke
another joint leaning against the precipitous slab
of the V-door, half-hitching quarter-inch wire
line under the shoulder and yanking the joint up
with power from the "air-hoist". They drop it
into the mousehole.

Then, most often, they can go to "the
doghouse" if they want, all the roughnecks,

shielded by sheet metal against smoking motors'
quaking and cable's screeches, or they can stay
out—maybe grab-ass in horseplay, maybe duck-walk
like on —The Gong Show—.
There's not much to do
Except bullshit
Before the next call.

Some Day

Up in the crown
To move its block with a "come-along"
One morning of March, late in a tower,
The demisted Gulf underneath
Platform and telescoped derrick
Such a shimmering and pellucid blue,
The derrick-man on A crew, me and Mike
Barnett—"Crazy Mike" from Oklahoma,
Who sledgehammered while hanging by one hand
From I-beams, whose T-shirt declared him a
Derrick Beast, "Daddy" at twenty-three
To a woman and three kids back home—
Talked about life from outer space,
This season of "Close Encounters ... ",
In a break we'd taken. Smoking, Mike
Looked at us suddenly. His smile was wry.
The visitors, coming down in their ships,
Would see all these rigs deserted, he
Imagined. "And they'll say:
"This is what killed 'em." "

March 19, 1982
First version 3/'80

Typesetting by Re/Search Typography